## Learning to Read, Step by Step!

**Ready to Read   Preschool–Kindergarten**
• big type and easy words • rhyme and rhythm • picture clues
For children who know the alphabet and are eager to begin reading.

**Reading with Help   Preschool–Grade 1**
• basic vocabulary • short sentences • simple stories
For children who recognize familiar words and sound out new words with help.

**Reading on Your Own   Grades 1–3**
• engaging characters • easy-to-follow plots • popular topics
For children who are ready to read on their own.

**Reading Paragraphs   Grades 2–3**
• challenging vocabulary • short paragraphs • exciting stories
For newly independent readers who read simple sentences with confidence.

**Ready for Chapters   Grades 2–4**
• chapters • longer paragraphs • full-color art
For children who want to take the plunge into chapter books but still like colorful pictures.

**STEP INTO READING®** is designed to give every child a successful reading experience. The grade levels are only guides; children will progress through the steps at their own speed, developing confidence in their reading. The F&P Text Level on the back cover serves as another tool to help you choose the right book for your child.

Remember, a lifetime love of reading starts with a single step!

*To Carla Hayden, Librarian of Congress—another stride forward*
*—V.M.N.*

*To those change agents who steadfastly affect their communities in even*
*the smallest simplest acts every day. March on!*
*—S.W.C.*

Text copyright © 2017 by Vaunda Micheaux Nelson
Cover art and interior illustrations copyright © 2017 by Sally Wern Comport

Visit us on the Web!
StepIntoReading.com
randomhousekids.com

Educators and librarians, for a variety of teaching tools, visit us at RHTeachersLibrarians.com

Library of Congress Cataloging-in-Publication Data is available upon request.
ISBN 978-1-101-93669-6 (trade) — ISBN 978-1-101-93670-2 (lib. bdg.) — ISBN 978-1-101-93671-9 (ebook)

Printed in the United States of America

10 9 8 7 6 5 4 3

This book has been officially leveled by using the F&P Text Level Gradient™ Leveling System.

Random House Children's Books supports the First Amendment and celebrates the right to read.

# DREAM MARCH

Dr. Martin Luther King, Jr.,
and the March on Washington

by Vaunda Micheaux Nelson
illustrations by Sally Wern Comport

Random House 🏠 New York

Everybody has dreams.

Some we share

with family and friends.

Some we hold in our hearts.

On August 28, 1963,
one man's dream was heard
across the nation.
When the Reverend Dr. Martin
Luther King, Jr., was a boy
growing up in Georgia,
he could not have imagined
a day like this.

People traveled from all over
the country
to Washington, D.C.
They rode buses, trains,
airplanes, and cars.
Some walked over 200 miles
from Brooklyn, New York.

One man rolled 698 miles

from Chicago on skates.

It took him ten days.

Over 250,000 people
gathered in the
nation's capital.

Singers, authors, actors,
government officials, and
other famous people attended.

But ordinary citizens
were the real stars of the
March on Washington for
Jobs and Freedom.

People packed
the National Mall
from the
Washington Monument
to the Lincoln Memorial.
Young and old of every color,
side by side,
hand in hand.

Many wore their Sunday best.

They carried signs.

They sang.

"I woke up this morning

with my mind set on freedom."

"We shall overcome someday."

Black people fought
for many years
for the right to be treated
with respect.
In the 1950s and 1960s,
black Americans organized
and fought extra hard.
Their fight was called
the civil rights movement.

Martin and others held
peaceful protests against laws
that kept black people and
white people apart.
They fought for the right
to attend the same schools
and eat in the same restaurants.

They fought to use
the same bathrooms
and drink from the same
water fountains.

WHITE

COLORED

They fought to sit

on any empty bus seat

and to have the same chance

at a job.

They fought for the right
to vote.

The protesters won
some battles,
and new laws made
things better.
But black people
were still treated unfairly.

In 1963, activists
A. Philip Randolph and
Bayard Rustin
and other civil rights leaders
decided to take the fight
to the nation's center of
power—Washington, D.C.

The march organizers
wanted to show
President John F. Kennedy,
Congress, and all Americans
how many people believed
in this cause.

The Declaration of Independence
says "all men are created equal."
The marchers wanted Congress
to make sure everyone
was treated that way.

United, they walked together.
Some were silent, determined,
intent, yet hopeful.

Most chanted and sang,

beaming, joyful,

their hearts light.

The marchers crowded
the Mall's Reflecting Pool.
Some took off their shoes
and socks to soothe their feet
in the cool water.
Others climbed trees
for a better view.
Lucky children perched
high on shoulders.

They looked toward

the statue of Abraham Lincoln.

It had been one hundred years

since President Lincoln signed

the Emancipation Proclamation,

which helped free the slaves.

Why were black Americans

not yet free?

27

President Kennedy
and other officials worried
that the marchers
might become violent.
Thousands of police and soldiers were
called out to keep order.

There was no need.

The March on Washington
was the largest human rights
rally in American history.
And there was no trouble.

Martin had one of the

strongest voices for

civil rights.

He had been jailed

for standing up for

black people.

His house was firebombed

by people who wanted him

to stop.

But he did not scare easily.

Martin was a minister.

He had faith,

and, wow, could he preach!

When Martin spoke,

it was as if he could read

the minds of people and feel

what was in their hearts.

Other leaders gave

inspiring speeches

at the march.

But Martin's words on that

hot August day made history.

In his speech Martin said
black people were tired
of waiting for their rights.

He said, "Now is the time"
for "justice."
"Now is the time"
for "brotherhood."

He said no one is free
until *everyone* is.

Martin spoke forcefully,
with grace and dignity.

His friend Mahalia Jackson,

the gospel singer,

called out,

"Tell them about

the dream, Martin!"

He put aside his written words.

"I have a dream," Martin said,

that "little black boys and black girls

will be able to join hands

with little white boys and white girls

as sisters and brothers."


Martin had a dream

that his children would live

in a country where they

would not be judged

by their skin color but by

"the content of their character."

Martin had a dream
that when children sing
"My country, 'tis of thee,
sweet land of liberty,"
the words ring true
for everyone.

He spoke of faith and truth,
love and hope.

Finally Martin said,

his voice like thunder:

"Let freedom ring!"

"From every hill" and

"every mountainside,"

"from every state and every city,"

"let freedom ring!"

And if we do, people

of all colors and all faiths

will join hands and sing:

"Free at last, free at last,

thank God Almighty,

we are free at last!"

Marchers cheered and cheered.
Some wept tears of pride,
joy, and hope.

They would never forget
this day.

Many who had been strangers

before the march

were forever bonded

by that moment in time.

People all over the country
watched the march
on television
or listened on the radio.
They felt the spirit
of the day, too.
They were reminded
that all people are meant
to be free.

Martin's dream
wasn't his alone.
It was a dream
millions of Americans shared.

Now his dream lives forever
in the hearts and minds
of people everywhere.
And the march for freedom
goes on.

## AUTHOR'S NOTE

Ten months later,

on July 2, 1964,

President Lyndon B. Johnson

signed the Civil Rights Act

into law.

It is unclear whether

the March on Washington

brought about

the passing of this bill.

But it was a step forward

in the civil rights movement

in America.